Bullfrogs *(Rana catesbieana)* are an exotic species in the Northwest. Some non-natives fit in well and enhance the environment; others do not.

Photo: Tim Fitzharris

Our thanks to many individuals for advice and help in the planning, funding and production of this book:

Ingela Abbott, Hilda Bajema, Sid Baron, Carl Batchelor, Steve Brinn, Mary Boire, Bill Carroll, Connie Clement, Joan Casey, Mike Conners, Sharon Digby, Richard Eggemeyer, Ann Eissinger, Jerry Eklund, Sheri Emerson, Alan Frazier, Bob Helsell, Virginia Herrick, Robert Janyk, Pat Karlberg, Lynne Masland, Bob Morse, Bob Myhr, Constance Pious, Bob Robbins, Gordon Scott, Bruce Smith, Doug Tolchin, Ron Vekved, Don Walter, Scott Walker, Scott Wheeler, Ken Wilcox

Book Committee:

Bob Keller, *chair.* Scott Brennan, Rod Burton, Julie Carpenter, Cindy Klein, Chris Moench, Patricia Nelson, Dave Peebles, Chuck Robinson, Duane Sweeney, Wendy Walker, Tom Wood, Ann Yow

PHOTOGRAPHERS

The Land Trust recognizes the important role of outstanding photographers in protecting nature. We are thankful for their cooperation in making this book possible.

Mark Bergsma
Brett Baunton
Matt Brown
Jon Brunk
M. Rodrigo del Pozo
Gene Davis
Jonathan Duncan
Tim Fitzharris
Sharon Eva Granger
Peter Kobzan
Lee Mann
Grant Myers
Tore Ofteness
John Pratt
Fredrick Sears
Sallie Sprague
Bob and Ira Spring
Mark Turner
Richard Williams
Ann Yow

Cascade foothills meet autumn woodlands along Goodwin
Road in northeastern Whatcom County.
Photo: M. Rodrigo del Pozo

ISBN 0–9657053–0–7   25.00

A SENSE OF PLACE

One dusk I squinted across the land where I was growing up and saw that the prairie is really a seascape.

The wind was blowing, as it did day and night that summer, and the moving waves of rich-yellow wheat could just be seen in the settling dark. A harvesting combine cruised on the far side of the field. I had never been within a thousand miles of an ocean, but I knew that the combine, with its running lights just flicked on, was a freighter bound through the night for Sydney. Bench hills rose to the north, surely a fair coastline. The expanse of it all, hills and fields and wind in the wheat, extended like an ocean to where the sky and the flat horizon fitted together.

The magic of place is indelible. I was fifteen, there at that found sea which was both fictional and real. Now at fifty-seven I write about both the Montana land where I grew up and the Puget Sound country where I have spent the majority of my years. Always I have believed that writers of caliber must ground their work in specific land and lingo in order to write of that larger country, life. So it is with us all, I would argue. Richard Hugo, the great poet of Montana and Washington, had a saying that sounded to me like something he picked up one especially grand night in a Missoula bar: "If you ain't noplace, you can't go nowhere." To have a base, a plot of accustomed existence on this earth, to be familiar with its changes of the seasons—there is propulsive rhythm to that. The ultimate experiencing of a sense of place comes from grounding our lives in such specific gifts of earth, and in having the sense to preserve them.

Ivan Doig

Whatcom County lies between two major river systems:
the Fraser (north) and Skagit (south) as seen in this Landsat
photo of Vancouver Island, the Strait of Georgia and the San
Juan Islands.

6

CONTENTS

The Whatcom Land Trust recognizes that people arrive at conservation decisions through diverse paths; therefore we have encouraged the authors in this book to draw upon individual experience and to express their personal convictions.

Mushrooms flourish in Whatcom County's temperate marine climate and are integral to nutrient cycles.
Photo: M. Rodrigo del Pozo

Whatcom County with Pt. Roberts in the upper left and the Cascade Crest boundary to the far right.
Map: Ken Wilcox

How we see Whatcom County depends on perspective. Here the Nooksack River flows from Komo Kulshan, "the Great White Watcher," spilling into a plain near Deming and Nugent's Corner.

Photo: M. Rodrigo del Pozo

Whatcom Places

Whatcom Land Trust

The most telling sign of old age is not caring anymore.

Anon.

"To enjoy a clear summer day like this in the mountains," she exclaimed on the trail below Austin Pass, "is worth all those months of clouds and rain!" Well, perhaps it's not paradise, but most people do agree that Whatcom County is a spectacular place to live.

Located between Seattle and Vancouver, B.C., Whatcom County with its relatively small 170,000 population offers a respite from the strain and stress of large cities. Its 143 miles of saltwater beaches and 3,000 miles of rivers and streams, its proximity to the San Juan Islands, and its backdrop of Cascade peaks make Whatcom a place cherished by residents and envied by visitors. This book, first and foremost, celebrates that landscape.

Beaches, lakes, mountains, islands and open space also encourage future growth and development. While rising population brings certain advantages, it also means changes in land use: some rural lands may become urban or suburban; open space will be more limited; agricultural land can transform into residential sites; low elevation forests may retreat and shrink; natural vistas of surface and sea can increasingly become scenes of human occupation and activity. We ask you to consider the challenges of such change.

Baker greets anyone looking east from British Columbia's Gulf Islands and Washington's San Juans.
Photo: Lee Mann

9

Old-timers and newcomers alike, whatever their politics or economic status, agree that Whatcom County today is an attractive place to live. Resort advertising speaks of "unspoiled shorelines . . . land left much as Nature created it . . . architecture that respects and blends with the pristine beauty of this dazzling region." Almost everyone agrees on what they like: it's not only jobs and a healthy economy, but the setting, public safety, quiet nights, fertile soil, clean air and water, easy access to trails and boating. Almost everyone wants to retain these treasures—but there is no consensus on how to do so. As is evident from the various voices in this book, people view Whatcom County from many perspectives, some compatible, some not. "Love for the earth," a Montana rancher has written, "is not exclusive to any class, occupation, or political persuasion." Facing our future thus requires an ongoing dialogue in public forums that include government, business, churches, special interests, commissions, the media. For some, there is also the forum of doing nothing. We address none of these venues here, except the last. Waiting and doing nothing is unacceptable if we hope to protect our heritage.

Whatcom Places advocates a particular type of action: the voluntary care of land by citizen groups, by business, and by landowners. A Land Trust member has succinctly defined stewardship as the responsibility of private landowners to care for their land. Aldo Leopold, the 20th century's premier ecological writer, expressed the same idea:

> *That land is a community is the basic concept of ecology, but that land is to be loved and respected is an extension of ethics. . . . Land is not merely soil; it is a fountain of energy flowing through a circuit of soils,*

The view from the eastern boundary of Whatcom County encompasses the Pasayten Wilderness, North Cascades National Park, Jack Mountain, Hozomeen, the Ross Lake National Recreation Area and Whatcom Pass, with Shuksan and Baker in the distance.
Photo: Grant Myers

Lake Whatcom and Bellingham Bay, two basins gouged by ice age glaciers, as seen from Stewart Mountain, east of the city.

The Nooksack River flows north below Sumas Mountain, west
past Everson and Lynden, then turns south through Ferndale
and Lummi Indian lands.

Photo: Grant Myers

plants and animals. . . . whoever owns land has assumed, whether he knows it or not, the divine functions of creating and destroying.

A Sand County Almanac (1948)

For Americans, part of our strong social fabric has always been voluntary ethical action by concerned citizens. When writing *Democracy in America* over 160 years ago, Alexis de Tocqueville observed that this "most democratic country on the face of the earth" was one in which its members eagerly joined together, outside of government and outside of their work, to promote and protect their common values. "Nothing," he informed Europeans in 1835, "is more deserving of our attention than the moral associations of America." We have maintained this tradition of voluntary civic responsibility through the Kiwanis and Rotary, through churches, garden clubs, civil rights groups, battered women's shelters, hiking organizations, nature advocacy groups, and numerous other associations. It is a crucial way of being patriotic.

Regard for this particular land, Whatcom County, can unite us to act beyond our own immediate self-interests, beyond our own temporary occupations. *Whatcom Places* honors beauty of landscape, fertility of soil, and the mystery of nature as seen by more than a dozen outstanding photographers; we hope they inspire a sense of belonging and respect for the land. The book acknowledges a few of the many caring people who have acted out of a generosity of spirit toward the future. And, finally, it seeks to capture a feeling for place—"if you don't know *where* you are, you don't know *who* you are"—and to convey the essence of patriotism, the love of one's homeland.

Point Roberts on Georgia Strait is cut off from Canada by a political quirk called the 49th parallel.
Photo: Tore Ofteness

Semiahmoo Bay and Spit, named for the Semiamu Indians, was the site of a boom town during the Fraser River gold rush of 1858.
Photo: Gene Davis

Five-acre Chuckanut Island is owned by the Nature
Conservancy. Its western cove is a popular landfall for kayaks
and canoes.
Photo: Gene Davis

Shorelines

Dave Peebles

On an October morning I crunch through gravel at Larrabee Park's Wildcat Cove. A woman bundled against the chill perches on a drift log, watching her toddler splash fistfuls of gravel into the water. Nudging heaps of eel grass aside, a beachcomber stoops to look for an agate or puzzle over a crab's moulted husk. I slide the kayak off my shoulder and onto the water, drop into the cockpit, and snap the sprayskirt around the coaming. I lean on the paddle and turn into open water.

A few brisk strokes bring me to rocks that lie a hundred yards offshore. From the west, a bruise of high cirrus spreads across the sky like an omen. The pale sun already casts a watery eye, anemic rays leaking through autumn's vapor-laden air. The warm-up uncongeals my blood.

At this stage of tide the kayak slips over a little tombolo or shoal between rocky outcroppings whose untold generations of crumbled shells have built a white beach. These rocks once joined the sandstone cliff, though imagination must stretch further to envision ancient processes that separated the rocks from the point, or formed the point itself.

As I turn northward, cabins as well as substantial homes dot the cliffs beyond the cove. The eye slides over most of these as unobtrusive details in a dramatic shorescape. Here and there a canoe or skiff lies across drift logs. A couple in an old plywood

Inland marine waters support complex ecological relationships among diverse life forms.
Photo: Mark Turner

Dave Peebles taught at Sehome High School for twenty-five years and is active in the Washington Water Trails Association.

rowboat back toward a buoy, the woman maneuvering with the oars while the man twists around to raise a crabpot.

A quarter-mile further north, Whiskey Rock reveals its former connection with Governors Point, a reef that lies exposed and unpassable at low water. Today the kayak crosses with room to spare, threading between barnacle-encrusted boulders. I watch for turnstones and harlequin ducks who favor such reefs for winter foraging. An occasional eagle surveys the scene imperiously. Great blue herons, ubiquitous on Whatcom coastlines, leapfrog along the shore until they tire of the game and circle around behind the advancing kayak. A seal pops up now and again, obsidian eyes like black portals into the void. An otter family at times will cavort here in boisterous waves, but today they attend to other business. The surge lifts me as gently as the breathing of a comatose giant.

Pausing to dwell on fantastic formations of sandstone cliff, I drift in close, press my palms against a sheer face or overhanging ledge, and scrutinize shapes and textures. My awareness turns to tectonic forces rumbling deep beneath the hull, to forces that thrust up Chuckanut sandstone for an interface with the sea.

Everywhere sea and land embrace. Shore configuration and bottom contours shape wave and current, which in turn sculpt the shore. Winter storms out of the southeast, or brisk northwest winds and "smoky southwesters" spilling out of summer's high pressure, hurl waves at Governors and Clarks points. These rebound sharply, creating steep "clapotis" that vanish in an instant as they meet the incoming sea.

The *ARCO Anchorage* passes Lummi Island en route to Cherry Point.
Photo: Tore Ofteness

Workhorses of the water, tugboats may be seen herding log booms or guiding supertankers past our shorelines.
Photo: Jon Brunk

16

The Port of Bellingham hosts freighters and passenger vessels from around the world.

Photo: Tore Ofteness

Waves shape any shoreline throughout eons of sheer relentless hammering, but something about these cliffs defies obvious explanation. The sandstone artwork that brackets Chuckanut Bay lies not where water presently meets stone but five to fifteen feet above high tide, the work of a sculptor whose dreams seem delicate, almost ethereal, not cataclysmic.

Mesmerized by this mystery, I count links back down the geologic chain. Prior to sculpting at different sea levels (a process ongoing even now, though at an imperceptible pace), before these beds uplifted and tilted, strata of sand punctuated by gravel beds were laid down in a basin or lake. Plant fossils show that Chuckanut sandstones were of freshwater or brackish origin. Tableaux of palm or tree fern trunks displayed in hollows at Clarks Point speak of a semi-tropical climate. A windstorm, flood or landslide buried these plants; perhaps they logjammed in the twist of a creek or sunk into the ooze of a bog.

Some beds accumulated sand, silt and gravel to thousands and even tens of thousands of feet. Such layers in turn were uplifted and folded by the very tectonic forces that fret and dream in fitful slumber under our homes and malls and highways. But geology's earth-scope can probe even further, producing a time-lapse movie reaching back beyond the building and eroding of mountain ranges to show a supercontinent breaking up, spinning off our North American fragment to embark on its own continuing westward trajectory across the face of the globe.

Shoreline paddling opens a window to the sea bottom. Deep purple sea stars and a scattering of their pale orange

George Garlick, a volunteer land steward for The Nature Conservancy, checks uses of Chuckanut Island near his home on Pleasant Bay.
Photo: Charles Nishida–courtesy of The Nature Conservancy

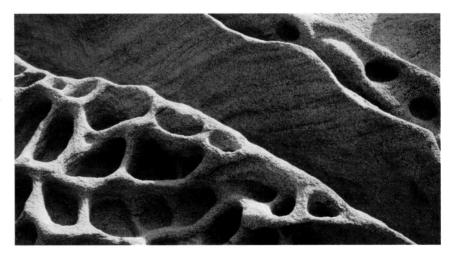

Centuries of water and wind have sculpted the Chuckanut sandstone cliffs at Larrabee State Park and Clayton Beach south of Bellingham.
Photo: Mark Turner

As on this island bluff, madrona trees are common along the western face of the Chuckanuts from Clarks Point to Blanchard—and are indicative of plant communities associated with the San Juan archipelago.

Photo: Gene Davis

Guests are welcome at the annual Lummi Indian Stommish
celebration in June. The event features canoe races among
tribes from British Columbia and Washington.
Photo: Sharon Eva Granger

Photo: Ann Yow   Juanita Jefferson
                                Lummi

Lummi traditional culture mixes with a modern tribal
government, casino, fishing industry, tribal school and
community college.

Photo: Sharon Eva Granger

*Lummi means both people and place, you can't separate
them. When we describe people, we describe where they come
from. We married outside our tribe, came together, and lived
in one place. That place was the identity you shared with
others. Al Charles taught me that my family extended over to
the Bellingham area, with blood ties to the Nooksack and
Semiamu people. This whole Whatcom County was possibly
our ancestral territory.*

*I was born in Whatcom, then left during the first grade, and
I always wanted to come back. I didn't like Seattle. I didn't
like the noise, the pushing and crowding, with concrete
everywhere and no trees. I wanted to return here, close to my
grandmother, a full-blood Lummi Indian whose teachings
were very special.*

*We used the forests and waterways to practice our spiritual
way of life. As those areas became more and more encroached
upon and destroyed, we moved higher into the mountains to
find clean, isolated areas. To this day our people go to Mt.
Baker for their spiritual life. Old growth cedar forest is what
they look for, and nowadays the mountains are even more
important for water. Our practices require clear, clean,
uncontaminated water and it's very difficult to find pure
water in lower Whatcom County today. The Nooksack River
has been contaminated badly by the time it reaches us, so we
travel up into the mountains. Land and water go together. To
us, they're equally important.*

Juanita Jefferson

morphs propagate along this rocky coast, as well as sea urchins and the occasional sea cucumber. Tiny pipe fish, related to sea horses, flutter like green ribbons, perfectly camouflaged by eel grass. Minuscule barnacles indicate high tide, the topmost fringe almost pioneers of air; a little lower their large relatives cluster in rockscape cities. Bladderweed drapes the barnacles at mid-tide, and, deeper yet, broad-leaved seaweeds of midnight purple shimmer with iridescence as if smeared with oil. Kelp crabs graze the canopy of this aquatic grove. I search pocket beaches and shallow coves for Dungeness crabs lurking in eel grass.

Beyond Clarks Point toward Bellingham I read a different story in a more recent chapter. Just south of Fairhaven the sandstone gives way to glacial deposits and alluvial benches. From here northward, our bays and coves are broad and shallow. Driven seas stumble across shoal bottoms and break into surf. Some bays become mudflats at low tide—poor timing at Drayton Harbor can strand the paddler in a morass of boot-sucking mud, pungent with anaerobic decay.

Rivers and streams partly account for the shallow Whatcom bays. Chuckanut Creek infills behind Burlington Northern's causeway. During heavy runoff the Nooksack River, and Whatcom, Squalicum, and Little Squalicum Creeks roil Bellingham Bay with sediments, requiring periodic dredging of the shipping channel. Unwary sailors have run aground nearly a mile off the Nooksack delta. Lummi Bay, a broad mudflat at low tide, is an offspring of the Lummi River, principal outlet of the Nooksack only a century ago. Terrell Creek contributes sediments to Birch Bay, while Dakota and California

"People's lives are immediately diminished whenever their connections with an elemental environment are blurred or broken."

Benton McKay, *The New Exploration* (1920)

Photo: Jon Brunk

Boulevard Park is part of a Greenways effort to protect a nature corridor along the marine bluff south of downtown Bellingham.

Photo: Courtesy of the Port of Bellingham

Local writer Tom Robbins once wrote of Pacific Northwest skies:
". . . and the sun is a little boiled potato in a sea of dirty dumplings."
Photo: Sharon Eva Granger

23

A county park at Teddy Bear Cove, property acquired through the Land Trust, provides access to the saltwater wonders of Chuckanut Bay. The Trust holds a conservation easement to insure protection of the beach and the Douglas fir slope above it.

Photo: M. Rodrigo del Pozo

creeks help clog Drayton Harbor. For places like these, slow death is inevitable.

Near Squalicum appear unmistakable signs of glacial deposition. The putty-colored bluffs along Eldridge Avenue, behind Little Squalicum Beach, and as far west as Cliffside are glacial till and outwash. These promontories of clay, sand, gravel and boulders erode inexorably into Sir William Bellingham's bay, augmenting the work of rivers and creeks. Portage Island's Point Frances, as well as bluffs along Cherry Point, Point Whitehorn, Birch Point and Point Roberts are similar, laid down by glaciers dating back 30,000 years and ending a mere 12,000 years ago.

A sudden swirl alerts the paddler along these points to submerged "erratics," granite monsters transported south from the Canadian coastal range on the backs of glaciers. Currents carry sediments from the eroding points to build spits at Semiahmoo and Sandy Point. Although piers and bulkheads blocking sediment flow can cause sandspits to vanish, the open deepwater industrial docks at Cherry Point appear to have not interfered with this process.

Glaciers acquire their burden by grinding down landscape. Whatcom shorelines testify to this as well. Off the western side of Lummi Island, Lummi Rocks bear a glacier's unmistakable imprint of long, parallel grooves inscribed into rock. I can trace them with a paddle from the kayak, or scramble onto rocks to reach other scars dozens of yards long, left by a juggernaut that engulfed the entire inland sea from the Cascades to Vancouver Island and the Olympics, overtopping not

Fern and palm fossils in Chuckanut sandstone tell of a tropical climate 65 million years ago.
Photo: Gene Davis

Migratory shorebirds, such as these western sandpipers *(Calidris mauri)*, find safe haven on Whatcom shorelines during their winter and spring travels along the Pacific flyway.
Photo: Tim Fitzharris

Shorelines

Water defines, enhances and sustains life.
Photo: Sharon Eva Granger

only Lummi Mountain, but Mt. Constitution on Orcas as well.

Paddlers poking along Whatcom bays encounter still another shaper of landscape, one whose urge to bend the world to his own ends has left significant, though scarcely eternal, marks. Within one short century many piers, canneries, log dumps and railheads have vanished except for scattered rotted pilings and twisted tracks. Tumbled slabs of broken concrete, rusted iron, and shards of brick—artifacts of human endeavors already faded from memory—form the "beaches" of Boulevard Park and outside Mt. Baker Plywood. Detritus we once hoped to forget bubbles up from the landfill beyond lower Cornwall Avenue, itself the result of dredge spoils dumped to reclaim a mudflat. Most of Whatcom County's salt marshes have given way to marinas, sewage lagoons and fill.

Threading between log booms in the Whatcom Creek waterway, I try not to spook sunbathing seals or sea lions draped over logs. From here I measure my kayak against ocean-going Foss tugs, watching from a safe distance as these little goliaths dodge and pirouette to nudge Russian or Chinese freighters into piers where they offload logs or accept aluminum. When an idle crew member waves, I lift my paddle.

After snooping into the dank underworld beneath Georgia-Pacific docks, I detour through Squalicum Harbor. Sailboats scurry out for an evening race, cruisers lay a course for the islands, purse seiners rumble by to stalk salmon. Kayaks co-exist easily with gillnetters, but must be more cautious riding a flood between the reef gear deployed in Legoe Bay. Near the shoals of Portage

The belted kingfisher *(Ceryle alcyon)* resides near lowland streams, estuaries, sloughs and lake edges. Dependent on fish, the kingfisher is most noted for its steep diving plunge in pursuit of quarry.
Photo: Tim Fitzharris

An icon of the Northwest, the great blue heron *(Ardea herodias)* thrives in lowlands where prime Whatcom County habitat supports the West Coast's largest breeding colonies.
Photo: Fredrick Sears

Commercial boats fish local waters or range as far as Alaska
and California in one of the few remaining hunter-gatherer
economies in North America.
Photo: Brett Baunton

Island, Lummi Indians stretch nets from the shore, and approaching Gooseberry Point I can dart behind the tiny ferry that shuttles islanders to and from their homes.

When I visit the still-wild parts of this shoreline, my first impulse is to think "timeless." Yet abundant evidence contradicts that delusion. Throughout our stretch of coast each place is caught in some particular moment and sign of transformation: cracks in cliffs that delineate future seastacks; hollows and honeycombs that are a mere gleam in the sculptor's eye; shattered sandstone eggshells that perhaps hatched behemoths a day before yesterday; silt-choked bays, moribund or already dead, whose rivers and creeks unburden cargoes of sand, the mud-mountains already piling up compound interest in sedimentary savings accounts; future sandstones prepared to lithify, uplift and wear down.

Our shoreline, together with all that mighty Cascadian upland that backs it, is but a grace note in the vast cosmic symphony—itself a work in progress. We, in our brief foray, dream that we possess it and mold it to our will. But we are at best transient stewards, often mere pillagers or interlopers, ever evanescent shadows . . . stardust.

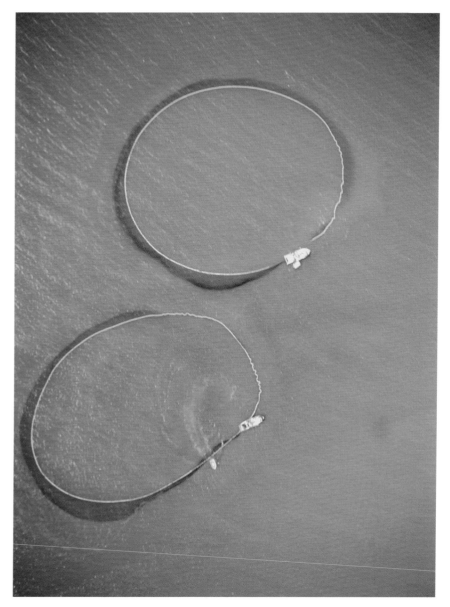

The herring roe fishery off Cherry Point finds a lucrative market in Japan and also attracts tens of thousands of migrating birds every spring.
Photo: Tore Ofteness

Shorelines

Reef net technology at Lummi Island was developed by
aboriginal people before European contact.
Photo: Sharon Eva Granger

Photo: Ann Yow

Tom Burton
Fisherman

You know, it's funny. I consider myself a trapper, I really do. I have a kinship with people who trap mammals for furs. I need to understand the animal that I'm hunting.

We don't celebrate individuality like we used to. We now try to homogenize and bring people into some sort of middle ground. That's unfortunate because you see the small farms going, the small logging operations, the small fishermen. Yeah, I feel a kinship with farmers and loggers.

Fishing? I love it. I love it! I'm never more alive than when I'm on the boat and off fishing. It's an honest occupation. You get what you put into it. And I love it here. When you're out on the water in the Georgia Strait and you see the Cascade Mountains, you see the island mountains, Baker's looming over you, the sun's shining, the water's sparkling, the air is clean, there's mammals in the water, some days we can see Mt. Rainier and the Olympics, it's just gorgeous. I wouldn't trade it for anything. Blaine is still a fishing community, you know. It still is, in its heart.

I think fishermen treasure water and land. Our livelihood, our success, our families' stability, come from our capacity to harvest in the wild in a sustainable fashion. The bulk of us respect those regulations. We realize that if we continue to take and nurture, and not be too greedy, the resource will continue.

Tom Burton

A resident harbor seal *(Phoca vitulina),* "hauled out," basks in the sun. Seals, cherished by most local citizens, are the only year-round resident marine mammals left in Whatcom County waters.

Photo: Fredrick Sears

31

A hiker can traverse Hannegan and Whatcom passes east to
Ross Lake. South of that trail is the Picket Range, with peaks
aptly named Phantom, Fury, Formidable, Inspiration and Terror.
Photo: Grant Myers

Rugged and Roadless

Wendy Walker

Beyond Mt. Baker, Whatcom County crumples upward into an engineer's nightmare of jagged peaks and deeply gouged canyons. Such terrain comprises more than half the county, stretching eastward fifty miles to a boundary in the Pasayten Wilderness called the Cascade Crest Trail.

Humans have yet to subdue this wild landscape. No roads penetrate the heart of the mountains, the only structures being fire lookouts and a few old mining cabins. The east remains a wilderness sanctuary, a thousand-square-mile undeveloped place that separates the towns and farms of the west from sparsely-settled ranching and orchard country in the Okanogan.

Eastern Whatcom County retains the character of a place newly born after millennia of glaciation. When mountains emerged from melting continental ice 10,000 years ago, bare rock provided an opening for new life to spin its web. Many of today's plants and animals belong to these pioneering young ecosystems. Alpine glaciers still carve the spires and ridges of the highest peaks. Meltwater streams cascade into primeval valleys thick with conifer forests which endure and even thrive despite 30 feet of winter snow, a two-month growing season, torrential rains and long droughts.

For much of the year, snow smothers this eastern half. Some places never lose their cold blanket, a glacial reminder that ice ages do return. Few humans venture long into the wild country

The mountain wildlife community is known for its distinctive characters: the whistling marmot, squeaking pika, majestic mountain goats and here, a ptarmigan *(Lagopus leucurus)* who relies on plumage as the best defense.
Photo: Grant Myers

Wendy Walker lives in Blaine and is a professor at Huxley College, Western Washington University.

Artist Point, at the eastern end of the Mt. Baker Highway,
provides breathtaking views of Shuksan (above) and Baker.
Photo: Grant Myers

Is all the effort worth it? Most hikers and climbers in the Cascades would answer with a resounding "yes!"

Photo: John Pratt

Climbers peer into a glacial crevasse on Mt. Challenger south of Whatcom Pass.

Photo: Bob and Ira Spring

Snowboarders and skiers enjoy some of the deepest and longest-lasting snow in the United States at Mt. Baker Recreation Area.

Photo: Peter Kobzan

"The charms of these mountains are beyond all common
reason, unexplainable and mysterious as life itself."

John Muir (1869)

Photo: Lee Mann

during winter's frigid temperatures and thunderous avalanches.

In the spring, as snow melts, the land softens and wakens to rushing streams and budding leaves. The short summer is halcyon and unrestrained as blooming wildflowers, clouds of insects and flocks of birds fill mountain meadows and forests. For a month or two, the high country becomes hospitable to mountain goats, marmots and humans.

Autumn's chill, sunny days bring vibrant reds and oranges. Blueberries ripen. Eagles, hawks and jays migrate south. Mammals hibernate or move to lower elevations as October winds bring early sleet and snow. Eastern Whatcom returns to its isolation.

Black bear, cougar and wolverine still inhabit these mountains through the cycle of seasons. A few grizzly may survive. Wolves are returning to the Cascades from Canada and wild salmon still spawn here. There may be animals in eastern Whatcom County who have never sensed a human, whose whole universe remains undisturbed by civilization.

Mountains that defy roadbuilding are an outdoor enthusiast's dream. Hikers enjoy a thousand or more trail miles; climbers scale peaks ringed by ice; kayakers, canoeists and rafters run untamed rivers. It's possible to live for weeks remote from any road. But our wildlands are more than playground. They offer renewal, mental and spiritual balance, a chance to rediscover challenges of living simply amid wilderness rhythms, the euphoria of knowing something more powerful and more profound than human affairs.

The Mt. Baker Hiking Club is Whatcom County's most venerable outdoor/conservation organization.
Photo: Courtesy of the Bellingham-Whatcom Co. Convention & Visitors Bureau

Imagine . . . . descending into brooding old growth, lying beneath a 1,000-year-old cedar, looking upward through gnarled branches at blue sky . . . . strolling an alpine meadow alive with butterflies and blossoms, sweet scents swirling in a summer breeze . . . . climbing sheer rock faces and finally standing exhilarated on the wind-blasted summit with a maze of crags in all directions. These too are Whatcom places.

Such natural areas sustain those of us who live and work in the western half. Mountains, among other things, determine weather, supply water and assist with waste removal; they contribute to air quality, hydropower, soil, biodiversity, pharmaceutical research, and global climates. The Cascades create weather by snagging Pacific storms: Huge masses of wet clouds roll in, slam into a barrier, rise, cool, and dump most of their moisture, much in the form of snow, on the western slopes. Accumulating during winter, melting during summer, glaciers and snowpack become reservoirs to sustain lakes, streams and people.

Early white explorers got it right when they called these mountains the Cascades. Waterfalls tumble down almost every cliff. Streams gurgle in almost every valley. It's hard to find a silent place in the North Cascades; water roars, crashes or trickles almost everywhere.

The Nooksack and Skagit Rivers collect their tributaries and head west and south, fluid transportation networks that bring drinking water and irrigation to numerous small towns. A minor diversion extracts power at Nooksack Falls. Three dams and a powerhouse—Ross, Diablo, Gorge, Newhalem—on Whatcom's portion of the Skagit account for much of Seattle's electricity. The

Maple Creek flows from Silver Lake, drops over Maple Falls, and enters the Nooksack.
Photo: Grant Myers

38

The Chilliwack runs north from headwaters near Hannegan and
Whatcom passes until it joins the Fraser River in British Columbia.
Photo: Mark Turner

Whatcom County's major river, the Nooksack, fed by snow and glacier-melt from the mountains, maintains a steady year-round flow.

Photos: Brett Baunton

Skagit below Newhalem remains freeflowing; the Nooksack is almost entirely free of human restraint.

For Whatcom County, the Nooksack provides scant hydropower, yet we are rich beyond our wildest dreams, or as rich as our dreams of the wild. We live within several hours' drive of swift rivers, ancient forests and impossible peaks: Mt. Baker Wilderness (122,000 acres), Noisy-Diobsud Wilderness (15,000 acres), North Cascades National Park (504,000 acres), Pasayten Wilderness (530,000 acres). It will require a long time for the Land Trust to acquire that much property. The wild, fortunately, is public. Each of us owns a share of:

** *hundreds of lakes*
** *millions of acres of forest*
** *countless streams and creeks*
** *an active volcano*
** *a thousand mountains*
** *hundreds of glaciers*

Every American shares this legacy, but we reside here. We are wealthy indeed.

With our riches comes special responsibility: to protect this heritage from abuse and from thoughtless human impact. We must invest in our future by being alert—acutely aware of the goals and actions of federal land managers and our local officials, men and women who will need our help in reaching decisions to protect these Whatcom places for centuries to come.

Mountains never teach apathy.

Once ranging from marine to mountain, the black bear *(Ursus americanus)* has become elusive and uncommon beyond the mountains. Bears symbolize wilderness and play a key role in the Cascade ecosystem.
Photo: Tim Fitzharris

Trails into Whatcom's high country above Ross Lake are reached mainly from Highway 20 via Skagit County and Newhalem.
Photo: Bob and Ira Spring

Diablo Dam blocks a deep canyon between Ross and Gorge Dams, part of Seattle City Light's Skagit River hydroelectric project.

Photo: Mark Turner

Glacial till or "milk" creates an emerald view for motorists at the Diablo reservoir overlook on Highway 20, with Colonial Peak in the background.

Photo: Grant Myers

From Lightning Creek Campground looking south down Ross
Lake: over millenia, this valley provided passage and sanctuary
for wildlife and people.

The Big Beaver Valley above Ross Lake contains one of the
Northwest's premier stands of old-growth cedar. When Seattle
City Light proposed raising Ross Dam and drowning this forest,
public protest saved the valley.

Photo: Lee Mann

Photo: Ann Yow

Tom Wood
Artist

I look to landscape as inspiration for painting. I like to be actually in it. Recently I've been sailing; I go out in the islands and find a place, camp out and paint. Painting's like fishing, sort of intuitive, where you get in tune with the place and then you can paint. It's not quick—every place has a spirit of its own, and you either know it or you don't. How much time you spend there makes a big difference.

Nothing is more special to me than my own area. All you can do is try to share your appreciation of a place with others. I guess because I'm outside and it's beautiful, that's why I do what I do.

Tom Wood

Forest Ruins–Noisy Creek
Painting: Tom Wood

What a paradise! Hikers can stroll through countless alpine
meadows in the high Cascades.
Photo: Grant Myers

Walking is just the right pace to appreciate the rich green texture of lowland forests.

Small pocket lakes exist throughout the Cascades. Some are easy trail hikes; others remain so remote and inaccessible that few fly-fishing addicts ever reach them.

For much of the year, clouds blanket the timberline forests of
the North Cascades.
Photo: Tore Ofteness

Kerry Thalhofer
Logger

"... knowledge of place comes from working in it in all weathers, making a living from it, suffering its catastrophes, loving its mornings or evenings or hot noons, valuing it for the profound investment of labor that you, your parents and grandparents, your all but unknown ancestors, have put into it."

Wallace Stegner, *A Sense of Place*

I got into the woods after college because there wasn't much else going on and I really enjoy it. I like working outside all the time. It's a challenge. There's always something out of the ordinary. It's a matter of coming up with solutions to problems that you just can't possibly foresee. You can't go out there and be fog-headed, you have to be awake all the time.

We started out with a skidder, then bought a shovel. Eventually we got back into cable systems, a small skyline thinning system so we can do partial cuts. It's a sweetheart of a system.

I enjoy thinning because it's more challenging, and when you get done, the forest looks like a park. Literally it does. We set out to do a better job without destroying things, to log it the way people want it to look. It's their property, but we want a final job we'd be proud of if it was on our own property.

Kerry Thalhofer

An opening in the foothills close to Saxon provides a glimpse of the Twin Sisters near a divide between the Nooksack's South Fork and the Samish River.

Photo: Lee Mann

Foothills

Binda Colebrook

Twenty miles east as the raven flies from the Strait of Georgia and Birch Bay, the northern-most Cascade foothills begin. This northeast area, which encompasses the towns of Sumas, Nooksack and northern Everson, lies in the Fraser River drainage. Here all water flows north via Sumas and Saar creeks, across the border, and into our Canadian neighbors' domain.

Frequently, however, the climate comes south. Hot, dry summer air flows out of the Canadian interior and overpowers the oceanic winds. In winter, freezing northeasters rage down the Fraser Canyon and into the valley, bringing snow, desiccation and a roaring as loud as a freight train. Dirt from cropless fields swirls in the air, giving a Gobi-esque quality to the scene.

Two northeast foothill sentinels, Vedder and Sumas mountains (the latter historically, and more rightly, called Nooksack Mountain), stand above the valley blocking winds, obscuring dawn and the eastern horizon, shining in the golden light of late afternoon, and dominating the entire day with an endless play of color, mist, clouds and vegetation. The two mountains are composites, scrapings off the oceanic plate: 65 million-year-old dinosaur-age sandstone; 100 million-year-old Mesozoic graywackes and shale; a scattering of 400 million-year-old limestone, chert and shale; and a serpentine metamorphic of indeterminate age that was once part of the ocean floor. The foothills stand like islands in a sea of glacial

Fifty years ago, few residents would have believed that wine-making would survive in northwest Washington's cold, damp climate. This popular vineyard on the Mt. Baker Highway comes alive every spring not only to survive, but to flourish.
Photo: Mark Bergsma

Binda Colebrook is an Everson writer and resident who specializes in native habitat restoration.

A unique wildlife conservation easement with the Trillium Corporation protects a bald eagle (*Haliaeetus leucocephalus*) night roost at Kenney Creek on the Nooksack River near its Middle Fork.

Above and left photos: Lee Mann

The Nooksack River's North and South forks join forces a mile upstream from Deming.

Photo: Mark Turner

Rain is much more frequent in Whatcom County than one might guess from this book. The sunlit drizzle in this scene near Potter Road, South Fork Valley, is closer to reality.
Photo: Mark Turner

outwash and recent alluviums. Barely 10,000 years ago, the receding edge of the most recent ice age glacier rose above the present town of Chilliwack, intermittently releasing its cargo of water-borne rocky debris out over the valleys of the Sumas and Nooksack rivers.

These outflows eroded long chains of wetlands that, in pre-settlement days, were filled with diverse native vegetation and huge noisy flocks of waterfowl so dense that local tribal people caught them by stringing nettle-twine nets between dead trees. In certain foothill pockets, large blocks of ice settled and depressed the land. This left kettle holes in which sphagnum moss and Labrador tea bushes grew and died for thousands of years, their acid layers creating a diary of changing pollen deposits and ash from volcanic eruptions.

Technically, northeastern Whatcom County is in the western hemlock/red cedar zone, but analysis of early surveys shows that about 37% of the land was periodically burnt over. The frequent fires created large patches of hazel and other shrubs scattered among dead trunks, young deciduous/conifer forests, and scrub-shrub wetlands. Where soil was too wet or too dry for trees, sedge meadows and grass prairies full of camas, Indian carrots and other flowers were maintained by the tribes. These fragile grasslands, a rare source of carbohydrates and medicinal plants, were quickly destroyed by plowing and free-ranging frontier hogs.

In the middle drainage of the Sumas River, across the present British Columbia border, lay a great shallow lake, ten miles by eight, but nowhere deeper than twelve feet. (*Sumaahl* means "big opening" in the Staalo's language.)

Sumas Mountain rises above farmland between Deming and Everson, providing a scenic backdrop for this chapel at Nugent's Corner.
Photo: M. Rodrigo del Pozo

Many rural residents come home from work to small farms. For some, horseback riding is a cherished sport.
Photo: Mark Turner

Around its edge grew a large bluejoint prairie, where first the indigenous peoples and then Euro-American settlers wintered their horses and hunted grouse. The lake, which increased to 30,000 acres with spring freshets, was known for its "wapato," or Indian potatoes, a plant now almost extirpated from Whatcom County wetlands. Here, too, was one of the great sockeye, sturgeon (and mosquito) breeding grounds of the Fraser.

The prairie was plowed and the lake drained in the 1920s, but the northwest face of Vedder Mountain still rises steeply from the valley floor. Those who hike or ride the logging roads gain marvelous views of the flat farmlands, Abbotsford, the trans-Canada highway, and the canyon of the Fraser as it heads east past Mt. Cheam and then into a vast northern interior. Wild creatures as well as people use this corridor. Western kingbirds, Swainson's phoebes and meadowlarks wing through from the east. Flocks of swans, grouse and ducks feed in flooded winter fields, and cougar, bear, elk, deer, beaver, muskrat and otter still inhabit the forests and river edges. The great wolves are gone. Only the omnivorous coyote, who arrived in their absence and ate the smaller foxes, howls at the edge of farms and suburban home sites. Gone, too, are the huge salmon runs, that incredible quantity of protein which once fertilized the stream beds and fed vultures, condors, eagles, crows and the many riparian mammals and invertebrates.

For thousands of years, ancestors of present-day Nooksack Indians occupied this area, harvesting protein from watery habitats, the burnt-over brush and deep forests. They climbed ridges surrounding Mt. Baker, seeking late summer berries and hunting goats whose

Not every town grows bigger with time. In 1910 Van Zandt on the South Fork was larger, and perhaps more lively, than it is today.
Photo: Courtesy of Duane Riddle

Trumpeter *(Cygnus buccinator)* and tundra *(Cygnus columbianus)* swans winter over in open farmland. The birds gain valuable sustenance from traditional crops and have increased in numbers due to protection.
Photo: Fredrick Sears

The Whatcom Land Trust works to conserve family farms and
the rich productivity of our agriculture.

Photo: Jon Brunk

Once considered useful only for "reclaiming," marsh lands
today are valued for water retention and purification, waterfowl
habitat, and a special calm beauty.
Photo: Gene Davis

Photo: Ann Yow   Susan Bennerstrom
Artist

Landscape is something that every human being can relate to because it's our mother. This is where we came from and it's what we're surrounded by, a never-ending store of ideas and possibilities for an artist. A painting covers time, too. Every second I'm working on a piece, changes are going on as I'm getting inside the thing. For me, painting covers more time and territory, internal territory, than taking a photo.

An underlying purpose of my landscapes is calling attention to and glorifying the mundane—to pay attention to what is extraordinary in the ordinary, like the way light hits the dirt.

Susan Bennerstrom

Lily pads at Lake Terrell
Painting by Susan Bennerstrom

This farm near Everson sells more than 200 varieties of fruiting plants.
Photo: Mark Turner

wool made prestigious blankets for ceremonial potlatches. To reinforce social ties and insure resource sharing, they married with the Lummi to the west, the Staalo to the north, and the Skagit to the south. Thus the large winter houses along the river edges heard bi- and trilingual conversations.

Now, dairies and orchards, small industries and suburbanites inhabit the valley floor. Nineteenth- and twentieth-century homestead families, loggers, farmers, newer professionals and vacationers have come to occupy the lower foothills. Second- and third-growth tree farms mix with clearcuts on private and state land. A few pockets of century-old forest survive, the large trunks and snags giving testimony to the past's immense cedars and Douglas firs. In amongst them grow the now uncommon smaller species of the understory. But, in the main, the hills today are covered with alder, birch and maple woodlands—beautiful and welcoming, yet only a hint of Whatcom's past, a landscape of memory.

Cattle, vegetables and fruit give Whatcom County a diverse agricultural base.
Photo: Mark Turner

Until recently, logging was a leading factor in the local economy. Many loggers have had to search for other jobs as forest resources dwindle.
Photo: Tore Ofteness

Foothills

Foothills carry a geologic and aesthetic message that rivals the
highest peaks and glaciers.
Photo: Grant Myers

Photo: Ann Yow

Kelsey Jack
Van Zandt, age 16

Protecting our family's land is more important for me than for my parents. I may live here a lot longer than they will—they've only been here 20 years. I might be here my entire life. And maybe I'm protecting it against myself.

I remember when Sunset Square used to be a field and trees, now it's in the middle of everything. I mean, it's really bad planning to put all those apartments on the outskirts of town. I'm afraid the city will spread way north and way east; it's spreading, spreading, spreading. It's going to keep on growing because it's such a wonderful part of the country and people will keep coming. As long as we have more and more people in the world, Bellingham will just keep spreading.

I've heard about cities building up instead of out. That's an idea people need to think about.

Kelsey Jack

Like the coyote, raccoons *(Procyon lotor)* adapt skillfully to human neighbors.

Photo: Grant Myers

People entered the Chuckanut hills south of town for food and timber, but few settled the rugged flanks. By the 1890s the trees had been cut. In 1904 a railway was blasted beneath the steep, porous slopes of Chuckanut sandstone, and three years later engineering genius once more challenged geology to complete a road that still clings to sheer rock the length of the range. This is Chuckanut Drive, a stunning if precarious auto route into Bellingham.

Deer, a few bear and cougar, many smaller mammals, fish and eagles still live in the Chuckanuts. The wolves have vanished, replaced by human homes on tree-clad peninsulas and higher slopes that command sweeping views of water, sky and islands. Trails open the interior to hikers. The former railway is now the Interurban Trail, a wooded artery into Bellingham by foot, bike or horse.

The Chuckanut hills today remain a place of forested beauty. Residents experience them as a way of life; those in Bellingham enjoy them when looking south. As new homes alter the land, geologists and residents ponder whether the Chuckanuts can safely support the changes on their steep and eroding slopes. What are the limits to traffic on the two-lane, cliff-hugging drive? What limit to removing trees for views of sea, islands, the Olympics? If everyone gets an unobstructed view, will the view be worth viewing?

Like most of greater Bellingham, Chuckanut's future invites debate. The Whatcom Land Trust considers the range valuable habitat for deer, racoons, eagles and— according to some—Bigfoot. In 1993, the Trust assisted the Department of Natural Resources, the State Parks and Recreation Commission, the Trillium Corporation,

To the consternation of rose gardeners and the delight of others, black tail deer *(Odocoileus hemionus)* still wander through the Fairhaven, Edgemoor and Sudden Valley neighborhoods.
Photo: Tim Fitzharris

Logging and home construction in the Lake Whatcom watershed contribute to ongoing disputes over preferred land use.
Photo: Richard Williams

"Dirty Dan" Harris in 1883 founded "Fair Haven on Harris Bay." Twenty years later the town had merged with New Whatcom and Sehome to form Bellingham, population 13,000.

Photo: M. Rodrigo del Pozo

Joe Bertero purchased a five-acre Bellingham truck farm in 1933. He still works in "Joe's Garden," now two acres larger, in 1997.

Photo: M. Rodrigo del Pozo

Foresight by our ancestors set aside city parks such as Lake Padden, which Bellingham residents still enjoy.

Photo: Jon Brunk

Whatcom County and the City of Bellingham in a major land trade. On Chuckanut and the hills above Lake Whatcom, 3,600 acres were exchanged for timber lands to the east. Washington's oldest state park, Larrabee, guarantees that some Chuckanut shoreline and forest will remain for the future. Several families have preserved their land. This includes a stream running through old growth; Teddy Bear Cove with its sandy beach; Dot Island just offshore from the Drive; and Clarks Point, a wooded finger of land on the northern curve of Chuckanut Bay. It's hard to imagine south Bellingham without these special places; they remain because private landowners vowed to keep them natural—for all to appreciate.

Chuckanut Drive brings residents and visitors into Fairhaven, a business district of old brick buildings and human-scale shops. The sandstone tideline stops here, replaced by structures of commerce and transport that cover the water's edge. Modern times have changed streams and forests too, but Fairhaven and Bellingham retain much of their original charm, thanks in part to people who volunteer time and labor to expand greenways, protect wildlife corridors, build trails and restore salmon habitat. There are community gardens, even a farm, in the city. Students at local schools take science outdoors to rehabilitate streams. Through its open spaces, Bellingham remains linked to less-developed areas: It looks, sounds and feels like a small city, but remembers its natural heritage in parks and greenways. People are drawn, rain or shine, to places like Lake Padden, sensing that space, trees and water are important, even crucial, to our well-being.

Pioneer days in Sehome meant stumps, mud and plank sidewalks. This view is north up Elk (now State) Street with woods beginning at present-day Maple Street. Wharf Street angles left toward the bay.

An Urban Future

The Whatcom Land Trust holds an easement that limits
development on 78 acres of private land at Clarks Point and
protects this scenic landmark. (The easement does not grant
public access.)

Photo: M. Rodrigo del Pozo

70

Photo: Jonathan Duncan

Doug Clark
Grocer

The Clark residence blends naturally into the landscape with a minimum of tree-cutting and is barely visible from the water or Chuckanut Drive.

Photo: Jonathan Duncan

South of the tunnel, 70-odd acres belonged to heirs of the Larrabee family. We paid $1,000 an acre for it. Everybody said, "You're nuts to buy that hunk of rock down there."

In 1958 my wife Peggy and I had been looking for something on the water. We looked all over—at Birch Bay, out at Lummi, down Chuckanut. We were coming back from Pleasant Cove and I looked over at a hill with timber on it and said, "What's over there?" This real estate guy said, "I know who owns it, and she'll sell it. Do you want to look at it?" I said, "Sure."

One day, thirty years later, Peggy and I were looking at it again from Chuckanut, at all the vegetation and wildlife habitat. We asked ourselves what would happen to this place in a hundred years. Would it all be cleared out with houses and concrete streets? We said, "What can we do to prevent that?" So that's how it started.

Then we began looking around for what to do. A city park didn't sound very good. I asked the mayor, Tim Douglas, if he had any ideas of what could be done with the property. He brought up this Land Trust deal—and brought Rand Jack in. A conservation easement sounded to us like the way to go to preserve it. We never regretted it. Our three kids were in favor of doing it, and my wife was really enthusiastic.

Doug Clark

Lost Lake in the Chuckanut Mountains is near the state's largest
public/private land transfer (1993) negotiated by the Land Trust.
Photo: Grant Myers

As Bellingham grows, residents grapple with how, where, and at what pace our city should develop. We find no easy answers—the diversity of Whatcom County means ongoing discussion over balances between urban and rural, natural and human, development and preservation.

Several lakes lie in the folded foothills east of the city. One distinguishes itself by size and importance. This is Lake Whatcom: nine miles in length, a mile and a half wide. The lake provides daily drinking and household water for some 60,000 people. Carrying water diverted from the Middle Fork of the Nooksack, the lake also supplies more than 35 million gallons each day to the Georgia-Pacific mill for pulp and paper production. Others use the lake for year-round recreation. An ever-increasing number want homes on its slopes and shores. A handful of houses dotted the lakeside in the 1930s; by 1995 there were nearly 4,000; present zoning allows 13,900.

For many Bellingham residents, Lake Whatcom is a large but often forgotten link to life. It is easy to ignore what flows from our taps and not remember that we are connected to the Deming Glacier and Park Butte. We tug at the lake from various directions for many different things which carry a price: drinking water, view homes, logging, motor boat recreation. Lake Whatcom, like the Chuckanuts, is a nice place to live that has limits.

A forested flood plain once stood north of the lake where a wild river made its way from glacier to bay. We have now tamed the Nooksack, the plain is farmland in

Sailboats are a less controversial recreational use of Lake Whatcom than motorized watercraft.
Photo: Jon Brunk

A waterfall, a fish hatchery, an educational facility and Maritime Heritage Park enhance public access to the mouth of Whatcom Creek near the Georgia-Pacific paper mill.
Photo: Mark Turner

Lake Terrell west of Ferndale offers boating and relaxation. An adjacent 20-acre gift to the Trust from Ruth Kelsey extends this refuge for waterfowl, raptors and mammals.

Photo: M. Rodrigo del Pozo

transition, and a growing town straddles the river at Ferndale. This fertile earth has grown food for generations and, as western Whatcom changes, the flatland transformation is especially obvious. Old barns sit in fields beside business parks. Malls and outlet centers spring up suddenly. In one glance we see agriculture, homes, industry, hotels, commerce, mountains and river— changes in part due to the land itself. No gulches or rocky bluffs impede construction here. Names like Bakerview and Grandview aptly describe the vista on clear days—it is spectacular. A few miles further west at Cherry Point and north at Birch Bay we find places just as stunning.

Whatcom, Chuckanut, Shuksan, Komo Kulshan, Nooksack, Samish —words that still whisper of a time before "Bellingham" or "Baker"—tell of peoples living here before us. We newcomers can appreciate ancient life-ways on this western edge, yet we have different habits. Forests, mountains, rivers and soil change decisively under our touch. Now is the time to ask: How much do we want to alter this land, this beauty? What do we want Whatcom County to look, sound and feel like?

From Chuckanut cliffs to Ferndale farmland, from Lake Whatcom to Bellingham Bay, in our city and county parks with the Cascades reigning over them, people benefit greatly from the land. And many offer their stewardship, giving with the taking, to sustain the splendor of our Northwest corner.

Students assist with stream restoration on Lincoln Creek.
Photo: Sallie Sprague

Volunteers restore salmon stream habitat near the ARCO refinery at Cherry Point.
Photo: Tore Ofteness—Courtesy of ARCO Cherry Point Refinery

Late afternoon sun highlights fall foliage above Boulevard Park
between downtown Bellingham and Fairhaven.
Photo: M. Rodrigo del Pozo

Phyllis & Charles Self
Newcomers–1987

We remember getting off the plane at SeaTac and being disappointed in the landscape. Just north of Everett we began to get some sense of the trees, but it really wasn't until we got to Chuckanut that it felt like the Northwest ought to be. It immediately felt like home.

We wanted to be on the water because there's a different feel on a coast and greater opportunities to explore. We found that here. Also, wherever we were, we wanted to return something. We felt a need, environmentally and socially, to be part of a community.

Once we bought the property, we trusted our builder, who had a strong sense of what's right for the land. And we intentionally set the house so it wasn't blocking any neighbors' views. Probably the one thing that makes the house fit in so well is leaving the trees, which gives us a much nicer perspective. We never thought of cutting down the trees; that was not a consideration. They're home to everything from eagles to hummingbirds. Trees represent the Northwest.

Phyllis & Charles Self

"Home, after all, is the place where finally we make our living. It is the place for which we take responsibility, the place we try to sustain so we can pass on what is best in it, and in ourselves, to our children." William Cronon

Our rich farm heritage provides self-sufficiency, a stable
economy and aesthetic land uses.
Photo: M. Rodrigo del Pozo

Loving the Land in Lynden

Ron Polinder

I grew up in the Lynden community. On second thought, I grew up when I moved away from Lynden. Not until my wife and I returned to rear our children, nearly 20 years later, could I articulate how this place and people molded me.

As a lad, I attended Lynden Christian School where it was our custom to do a good bit of singing when the school day began. I now realize how songs from that old red songbook imprinted my basic values. Like "The Seed Song," No. 21. On the opposite page was the darkened silhouette of a farmer riding a sulky plow behind a team of horses. We sang:

See the farmer sow the seed / While the field is brown;
See the furrows deep and straight / Up the field and down.
Wait a while and look again / Where the field was bare;
See how God has sent the corn / Growing golden there.
CHORUS: *Farmer, farmer, sow your seed / Up the field and down;*
God will make the golden corn / Grow where all is brown.

I liked the song and the picture that went with it—they spoke to me.

Just what, one might ask, did the song say? Simply put, it reminded me that God had a whole lot to do with what happened on our family farm. In one way or other, most of us who grew up near Lynden got that message. It may have

Lynden's traditional Dutch culture is more than decor: It has its roots in religion and a land ethic.
Photo: Courtesy of the Port of Bellingham

Ron Polinder is principal of Lynden Christian High School and lives on a 14-acre farm along the Nooksack.

come from the pastor's sermon, or the Prayer Day service, or the Harvest Dinner, but we learned that farming was sacred, not unlike going to church or school. All of life related to religion. "Secular" was not a word in our vocabulary.

And therefore the milk that poured into the tank, the oats that poured into the combine, the strawberry jam that poured into canning jars, all were a blessing released from the bounty of God's storehouse. We had been placed by God's good providence in a land of plenty. We lived along a river, the Nooksack, where "river bottom" soil was dark and rich. We counted it a privilege to live there even when floods put us to the test—diking and ditching.

We also admired people north of Lynden on a rich flat plain sprinkled with well-kept family farms. Berry growers west of town were likewise honored. We would U-pick a few mornings every summer, marveling at the beauty of red ripe berries. And my mother would invariably chat with the owner or field boss who hoped to find enough pickers to harvest the fruit and make a decent profit.

Lynden meant farming. Townspeople realized that their livelihood was closely linked to an abundance that came from the soil. They went to Prayer Day services; they made themselves available when you needed extra hands for haying or sandbagging.

Life in Lynden in the '50s had a routine, rhythm and richness that provided security, identity and community. Mine was a privileged childhood, not because we were wealthy or free from problems, but because, bound

Agricultural land, midwestern in tone and feel, adds to Whatcom County's variety. And here, as elsewhere, the transition from family farm to industrial agriculture tests a conservative land ethic based on direct individual ownership.

Photo: Tore Ofteness

A Lynden plowing match occurs every April. Attention to our heritage is also possible at various local museums, the Peace Arch in Blaine, Berthusen Park in Lynden and Hovander Homestead Park in Ferndale.

Photo: Mark Turner

Technology allows economic survival but also changes the
scope, human scale and meaning of farm life.

Above and above right photos: M. Rodrigo del Pozo

". . . Hatsue wanted only her own strawberry farm, the
fragrance of the fields and the cedar trees, and to live simply in
this place forever. . . . If identity was geography instead of
blood—if living in a place was what really mattered—then [this]
was part of her as much as anything Japanese."

David Guterson, *Snow Falling on Cedars*

Photo: Mark Turner

82

together by faith, family and friends, we knew who we were and from whence we had come.

The 1960s drew many away, in my case to far-off Calvin College in Grand Rapids, Michigan. The '60s tumult did not fully reach conservative colleges for another decade, but revolutionary ideas were in the air. It was a marvelous time to be a liberal arts student, to be exposed to the complexity of life and learning, to be challenged regarding the simple answers that accompany youthfulness. As a history major I learned that ideas have legs—they lead somewhere. I began to comprehend the Enlightenment, the Age of Reason, the advance of modern science and technology, our division of life into sacred and secular. Privatized religion left theology little to offer politics, education or science. We came to see how the rise of secularism subverted a theistic world view, a way of life.

Which brings us back home to Lynden and its agricultural community. Did secularism overwhelm the faith of the '50s where we started? As science and technology change the face of farming, does it become easier to trust irrigation systems rather than the prayer service? Have chemicals and fertilizers replaced the faith and hope that previously guided our relationship with the earth? Does any theology or ethic undergird modern agribusiness and land use, or are these "secular" activities?

I cannot begin an answer, for the answers lie in the hearts of hundreds of individual farmers. But I do confess to fretting about it. I want to live a theology that unites faith and farming, a Creator of the universe with the Creator of science, the Lord of the Scriptures with land use in the '90s.

Despite modern invention, farms such as this one on Northwest Road offer the experience of an ancient harvest method.
Photo: Mark Turner

83

Perhaps this can be best illustrated by the story behind the Whatcom Land Trust. This organization did not begin at Huxley College of Western Washington University, or as an offshoot of the Democratic Party, or the brainchild of an environmentalist from Fairhaven. The Whatcom Land Trust was conceived in the basement of Dutch Mothers Restaurant, downtown Lynden. In 1983 Concerned Christian Citizens, having an interest in farmland protection, was contacted by the Trust for Public Land. A forum in cooperation with TPL attracted nearly fifty people, including County Councilman Bob Muencher, Trillium founder David Syre, attorney Rand Jack, stewards like Hilda Bajema, farmers like Herman Miller. Group chemistry insured more discussion; eventually the Whatcom Land Trust was born. As executive director of Concerned Christian Citizens at the time, I have found the ongoing work of the Trust a source of considerable satisfaction.

But why would Lynden-based Concerned Christian Citizens be the origin of this movement? History provides the answer. Though not founded by Dutch immigrants, Lynden was discovered by them around 1900. They brought here a sturdy Calvinsim which immediately gave birth to Reformed churches and, as early as 1910, Lynden Christian School. Their Calvinism emphasized the sovereignty of God over all of life, or as Dutch theologian and Prime Minister Abraham Kupyer once said: "There is not one square inch of the entire creation about which Jesus Christ does not say, 'This is mine! This belongs to me!'" Psalm 24 claims, "The earth is the Lord's, and the fullness thereof." The Creation was God's handiwork and he placed Adam and Eve in the

Herman Miller, a Trust founder.

The Whatcom Land Trust's first conservation easement (1986) protected the 160-acre Miller farm.
Photos: Mark Turner

It is possible to develop and use land without destroying our sense of scale and belonging. Various books can guide us in fresh thinking: *A Place in the Islands* by the San Juan Preservation Trust; *Rural by Design* by Randall Arendt; *A Pattern Language* by Christopher Alexander; and *The Experience of Place* by Tony Hiss.

Photo: M. Rodrigo del Pozo

"We need an environmental ethic that will tell us as much about *using* nature as about *not* using it . . . some kind of responsible use and non-use that might attain a balanced sustainable relationship."

William Cronon, *Uncommon Ground* (1996)

Photo: Jon Brunk

garden "to work it and take care of it." (Gen. 2:15). John Calvin's commentary on Genesis elaborated: "Let him who possesses a field so partake of its yearly fruits that he may not suffer the ground to be injured by his negligence, but let him endeavor to hand it down to posterity as he received it, or even better cultivated . . . let everyone regard himself as a steward."

There we have it — a concept of stewardship. The Christian community today has rediscovered precisely this concept in the wake of the environmental crisis. For example, the book *Earthkeeping* (1980) provides a theological framework for applying Christian faith to ecological issues.

But has this "intellectual" framework for stewardship reached the farm or infiltrated conversations in the coffee shop? Is it merely a worldview, not yet a way of life? Has secularism won in everyday life, making us practical atheists? What theology sits in today's tractor seat?

Bertrand Russell once spoke of a simplicity on the other side of complexity. Lynden started with simplicity and moved into the complexity of "progress." I wish for my community that we might collectively find that second simplicity, a simplicity on the other side of complexity, a simplicity captured in another song (from that old songbook) and in a prayer.

"This is our Father's world: O let us not forget that though the wrong is great and strong, God is the ruler yet. He trusts us with this His world, to keep it clean and fair — all earth and trees, all skies and seas, all creatures everywhere."

Father, I pray for my community, all my friends and fellow citizens, that we will do justice to the land, to

Guide Meridian in 1908.
Photo: Courtesy of the Whatcom Museum of History and Art

Agriculture adds its own ordered beauty to Whatcom County.
Photo: Matt Brown

the creatures, to all. I pray for an ethic that will move us to be stewards of the earth. I pray for a grateful heart to appreciate this wonderful place in Creation called Whatcom County and its smaller part called Lynden.

Thank you for productive cattle and graceful horses that feed on and run through our pastures and for each lovely critter that makes up the web of life. Thank you for corn choppers and computer chips, tools you have provided to take away the drudgery of work. Thank you for the geneticist, the chemist, the agronomist who uncover the intricacies of Creation and use their knowledge to redeem life and culture. Father, if we have to build bigger barns, would it not be for greed or ego! Would you prevent us from always bending our knee to the market, treating it like it is God. Would you spare the family farm in this community.

Father, make us aware of any abuses we engage in, polluting our water, spreading too much manure, using too many chemicals. May we know when our profits are enough, when we have worked enough, when we have saved enough. Help your stewards know when we have been negligent, unobservant, or disobedient.

Father, deliver us from any thought that we are on our own, that you have deserted us, that we can do this without you. We simply acknowledge you as the Creator of "all things bright and beautiful, all creatures great and small, all things wise and wonderful, Lord God, you made them all." AMEN

"All nature—even human nature—begins and ends with the land."

Trust for Public Lands

Facing and above photos: M. Rodrigo del Pozo

89

Summer hay in the loft will feed Holstein cattle on this
Whatcom dairy farm over the winter.

Photo: Jon Brunk

John, Ben & Karen Steensma
Dairy farmers

This familiar creature, the short-eared owl *(Asio flammeus)*, is the farmer's ally in helping to control rodent populations.

Stewardship is taking care of God's creation for future generations. You try to keep it close as possible to how you found things, or improve it. We hope one of our kids will stay here and that a farm community will survive for a long, long time. This is good farm land and shouldn't be paved over.

This was my grandparents' place. Today you usually don't just go out and start farming, you have to be born into it. I always wanted to work for myself, and I like being outside with the cattle, watching things grow. Since I've been four years old, I've been fascinated with things growing. Besides, if you farm good land, you've got a job forever.

Because of our climate, this is one of the best places anywhere to make milk or grow berries. There've been times in the past when Whatcom County had the highest per-cow milk production of any place in the world. It's still in the upper five percent. But if people keep pulling out, we're going to lose the critical mass to maintain a farming community.

And if everything is created by God and has its place, and it's good in its place, then we can't claim the only motive is profit and the good of man. All the creatures, all the plants, have a specific place. Land's not just there for us. You can go into the environmental stewardship thing from a Christian perspective, and maybe that's a stronger reason to be concerned than for someone who is a secular environmentalist.

John & Karen Steensma

Tom and Ingeborg Nesset placed a conservation easement on their 100-acre homestead farm and provided for the land to become a county park.

Photo: Rand Jack

Stewardship, Conservation Easements and the Landowner

Rand Jack

". . . to preserve and protect the unique natural, scenic, agricultural and open space land in Whatcom County through the acquisition of perpetual conservation easements or other land interests that will insure protection of the resource."

Whatcom Land Trust Mission Statement, 1984

This is the challenge of stewardship: How do we account for our impact on something much older (and perhaps much wiser in its ability to sustain itself) than we are, something that will be here long after we are gone? Something upon which we and future generations ultimately depend for much of our well-being: the land. The land not in the sense of soil, but as an integrated biotic community rooted in the soil, a web of living things.

We depend on the land as a productive living community, not only to provide food and wood fiber, but also to give us clean air and water, to sustain climate, maintain the carbon cycle, and to sustain its own health. Given this dependence, it is incumbent upon us to care for our land. This relationship of care is called stewardship.

To own property means we gain a basket of rights with regard to our property—the right to build a house, to have a picnic, to mine for gold, to plant trees, to cut trees, and so

Tom Nesset (1898-1992), born in Norway, moved to his family's South Fork farm at age three and lived there for the rest of his life.

Photo: Rand Jack

Rand Jack, an attorney and university professor, has handled major land transactions for the Whatcom Land Trust.

on. The Land Trust's job is to help landowners conserve the habitat, scenic, agricultural and open space qualities of their land.

The government may take away certain landowner rights through zoning and land-use regulation. Local government, for instance, may prevent you from filling wetlands, building an apartment, or subdividing your land into parcels smaller than one acre. Landowners may also give or sell some of their rights to others, such as a right to build a road across the land or a right to remove gravel. *Conservation easements* offer another alternative by which landowners may voluntarily give up specified rights in order to conserve valuable qualities of their land. For example, if a property owner wishes to conserve habitat for pileated woodpeckers, the owner might use a conservation easement to limit cutting of snags and trees or to restrict the number of buildings.

The Land Trust works with landowners to assess special qualities of their land and how those qualities might best be conserved. Often a conservation easement is the most effective tool for doing so. It is a private agreement between a landowner and the Trust whereby the owner gives up carefully specified rights in order to accomplish open space, agricultural, scenic and habitat conservation goals described in the easement. Each easement is completely voluntary and tailored to the wishes of the landowner, the qualities of the land, and the goals of the Trust. An easement cannot be created until an owner and the Land Trust agree on the conservation goals and how they will be accomplished.

Urban paths and wooded drives such as this highlight a quality of life that attracts visitors and residents to the county. The Land Trust owns a 16.5-acre wooded wetland adjacent to the popular Interurban Trail in south Bellingham.

Photo: Lee Mann

Under a conservation easement, the Land Trust becomes the guardian of any rights given up by the landowner. Unlike the recipient of an easement to cross someone else's land, the Land Trust holds the rights of a conservation easement "in trust" and cannot actually use them.

After signing an easement, the owner still owns the land. It may be sold or left to heirs, but the restrictions remain with the land in perpetuity. The Land Trust is responsible to see that owners comply with these restrictions in the future. Because of this responsibility, the Trust asks easement donors to make a cash gift to a fund used to monitor compliance with the agreement. If this is not possible, the Trust may in some instances undertake to raise the monitoring contribution from other sources.

The Whatcom Land Trust is a 501(c)(3) nonprofit corporation. Your donation may create income, estate or property tax benefits.

If you are interested in stewardship possibilities for your property, contact the Whatcom Land Trust at (360) 650-9470.

WHATCOM LAND TRUST

Production Notes

Design: **Roderick C. Burton–Art & Design**

Body text and headlines are set in Minion, captions and credits are Syntax, supplementary type is Ellington.

Pre-press assistance: **Pyramid ImageLab**

Scanning: **DPI/Digital Photo Imaging**

Scans done using a Scanview 4000 drum scanner or Nikon Cool Scan.

Printing: **Premier Graphics**

Printed with vegetable-based inks on Vintage Remarque Velvet Dull 100# text with matching cover. Recycled content: 50% (10% post-consumer waste)

"Until I was thirty, I wanted to save the world. Between the ages of thirty and sixty, I wanted to save the country. But since I was sixty, I've wanted to save the Indiana Dunes."
U.S. Senator Paul Douglas.

In the Northwest, our "dunes" are natural treasures like Chuckanut Bay.

Photo: Jon Brunk

Conservation Futures levy money and a large private donation through the Land Trust enabled Whatcom County Parks to acquire Squires Lake. A conservation easement insures low human impact.

Photo: Mark Turner

Back Cover: Whatcom County travelers have discovered images of Mt. Shuksan from Picture Lake—considered the most photographed view in the world—in Africa, India, Israel, Germany and the Swiss Alps.

Photo: Mark Bergsma